W9-BBY-686

Mr. Jawahar K. Kaliani
2504 Crystal Tree Drive
Champaign, IL 61822

The KidHaven Science Library

Microscopes

by Gail B. Stewart

KIDHAVEN PRESS™

THOMSON
GALE

San Diego • Detroit • New York • San Francisco • Cleveland
New Haven, Conn. • Waterville, Maine • London • Munich

THOMSON

✦ ™

GALE

© 2003 by KidHaven Press. KidHaven Press is an imprint of The Gale Group, Inc.,
a division of Thomson Learning, Inc.

KidHaven™ and Thomson Learning™ are trademarks used herein under license.

For more information, contact
KidHaven Press
27500 Drake Rd.
Farmington Hills, MI 48331-3535
Or you can visit our Internet site at http://www.gale.com

LIBRARY OF CONGRESS CATALOGING-IN-PUBLICATION DATA

Stewart, Gail B., 1949–
   Microscopes / by Gail B. Stewart.
      p. cm. — (The KidHaven science library)
  Originally published: San Diego, CA : Lucent Books, © 1992.
  Includes bibliographical references and index.
  Summary: Discusses the history, development, and future of the microscope.
    ISBN 0-7377-0945-6 (hardback: alk. paper)
    1. Microscopes—History—Juvenile literature. 2. Microscopes—Juvenile
literature. [1. Microscopes.] I. Title. II. Series.
    QH278.S74 2003
    502.8'2—dc21

                                2002015269

Contents

Limits

It is hard to imagine that science existed before there were microscopes. Of course, there was science; there have always been people interested in exploring and learning about how nature works. However, those long-ago scientists had to do their exploring with their unaided eyes.

They did not know about the tiny details of the things around them. They could not see the amazing designs on the wings of a fly. They could not see that a drop of pond water was actually home to many tiny animals.

Doctors could not see the germs or viruses that made people sick. And because they could not see such things, they did not understand disease. Some scientists believed it was a punishment from God. Some believed disease was the presence of an evil spirit. Yet a few doctors wondered if there was a natural cause of disease. But because they had no proof, they were not taken seriously.

However, the microscope changed science. In the hands of scientists, microscopes opened up a world

A student studies a butterfly under a microscope.

that previously had been invisible. Microscopes have allowed scientists to better understand the nature of living things. Excited by what they were learning, scientists developed bigger and better microscopes. Researchers today are still trying to see more, with many new types of microscopes. As a result, more and more invisible worlds are coming into focus.

Chapter 1

The First Microscopes

The earliest microscopes were built during the late sixteenth century. Long before then, however, people knew it was possible for an object to be magnified—that is, to seem larger than it is. For example, water could magnify things. A raindrop falling on a tiny insect made it appear larger. Viewing a piece of paper through the bottom of a glass of water made the individual letters seem larger, too.

Bending Light

People noticed that certain solid materials were magnifiers, too. Nero, an emperor of ancient Rome, found that things were magnified when he looked at them through a large curved jewel called an emerald. Others found that curved glass could produce the same result.

For many years, no one was sure how magnification worked. However, in about A.D. 1000 an Arabian mathematician named Abu Ali al-Hasan ibn al-Haytham figured it out. He worked with lenses, or curved pieces of glass. He realized that the curves

The fine details of a snail's shell are captured under a magnifying glass.

actually bent the light waves as they traveled through the glass. When that happened, the light would make an object look bigger. Over the years, other scientists studied different lenses and learned how to grind them in certain ways to make them into magnifiers.

These early lenses were not powerful magnifiers. In fact, many people used them as eyeglasses for reading and other close work. But gradually, some of the lens grinders became very skilled. They experimented with lenses with greater curves. Some of these could magnify objects four or five times. These were too powerful to be used as eyeglasses. Without realizing it, these lens grinders had invented the microscope—in its simplest form.

Simple Microscopes

In fact, by the fifteenth century, people were already calling these magnifiers microscopes. The word *microscope* is a combination of two Latin words: *micro*, meaning "small," and *scopos*, which means "to look at." These early magnifiers did not look at all like microscopes of today, however.

A magnified view of a head louse. Today's microscopes are much more powerful than the simple microscopes used in the fifteenth century.

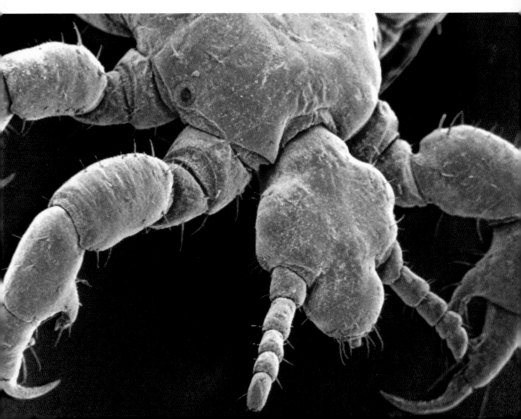

These **simple microscopes** had one glass lens. They were small, too, measuring only about two or three inches long. Some of these simple microscopes looked like tiny telescopes. They consisted of tubes with a curved glass lens on one end and a flat clear piece of glass over the other. To use one, a person would hold the microscope against one eye and hold the object to view in the other hand.

Other simple microscopes were built to be used on a desk or a table. They were made by mounting a lens on a wooden stand. An arm connected to the stand held a sharp rod, which held the object to view in place. This was a convenient design because people's hands would be free to draw or write about what they saw.

Both styles of simple microscopes were popu-

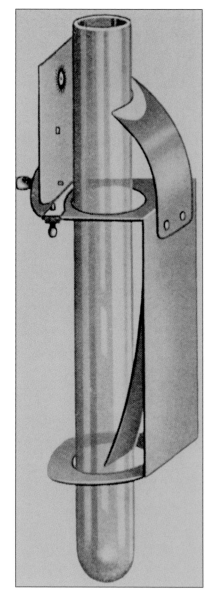

An engraving shows that one of the first simple microscopes looked similar to a tiny telescope.

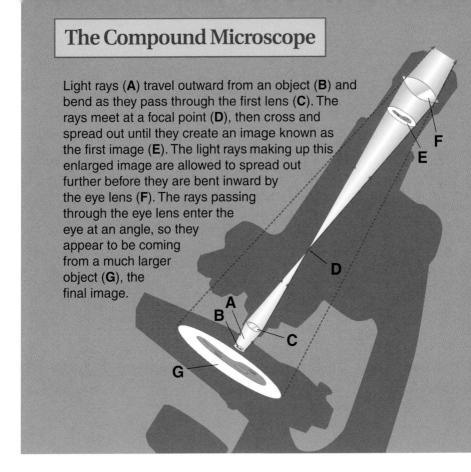

The Compound Microscope

Light rays (**A**) travel outward from an object (**B**) and bend as they pass through the first lens (**C**). The rays meet at a focal point (**D**), then cross and spread out until they create an image known as the first image (**E**). The light rays making up this enlarged image are allowed to spread out further before they are bent inward by the eye lens (**F**). The rays passing through the eye lens enter the eye at an angle, so they appear to be coming from a much larger object (**G**), the final image.

lar during the 1500s. They took a long time to make, however, for a craftsperson had to grind and polish each lens by hand. For that reason, microscopes were very expensive. Wealthy people often bought them, looking at the microscopes as fascinating toys.

The Compound Microscope

Over the years, these microscopes were improved. For one thing, glass makers created clearer glass with fewer flaws. Lens makers became more skillful, too. They could create lenses that were polished and ground smoother than ever before. The base of the

A fly's head is magnified thirty-nine times. The compound microscope had two lenses and was able to magnify objects multiple times.

table microscope was also improved. Inventors found a way to make the base swivel so that a scientist could adjust it more easily.

Scientists had wondered if they could create a more powerful microscope with two lenses, instead of one. In 1590 a father and son team of lens grinders,

Hans and Zacharias Janssen, tried to do just that. They built the first **compound microscope**, so-called because it had two lenses. One lens was **concave**— thin in the middle and thicker at the edges—and the other was **convex**—thick in the middle and thin at the edges. Using both lenses, a person could magnify an object nine or ten times—about twice as much as a simple microscope.

Flies as Big as Lambs

One man was excited by the images he saw. He told a friend that he had seen flies through the compound microscope that looked as big as lambs. Another noticed the designs on a moth's wing and the hairs on the legs of bees. These details had been invisible before, even under the simple microscope.

The compound microscope was popular with wealthy people, just as the simple microscope had been. By 1625 so many people wanted to own compound microscopes that microscope shops were located in almost every city in Europe. Some microscopes were very fancy, with leather covers and gold decoration. However, they were no longer merely toys. Scientists realized that only with a microscope could they see these fascinating new worlds.

Snowflakes, Fleas, and Cells

One scientist who recognized the importance of this new tool was an Englishman named Robert Hooke.

Hooke had made improvements in his own microscope, and he was able to magnify objects up to thirty times. That earned Hooke the respect of fellow scientists. But what impressed them even more were the drawings he had made.

Hooke was an excellent artist and had made detailed drawings of things he had seen with his

Robert Hooke drew every detail of a flea viewed under his microscope. Today, a flea's detail (pictured) can be captured immediately.

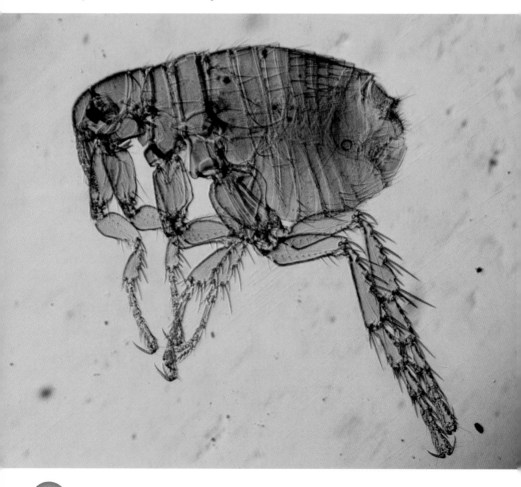

microscope. As he showed them at a 1662 meeting of the Royal Society, one of England's best-known science organizations, the other members were fascinated. Here were details they had never seen in their studies. There were snowflakes, each with an intricate design, and fleas, which looked frightening in their detail.

One of the drawings that amazed the other scientists was of a piece of cork. Hooke noticed that cork was made up of what seemed like millions of tiny divisions. They reminded him of little rooms, or **cells**. Hooke gave these divisions the name *cell*. That word is used today to describe the units that make up all living things.

Hooke later assembled many of his drawings in a book. He called it *Micrographia*, which means "small drawings." He was considered a genius for his work. Most important, his work was a reminder to other scientists that there was a great deal to learn about the world. And the microscope would be the tool to help them learn.

Animals in His Mouth

The things Antonie van Leeuwenhoek saw with his microscopes were just as amazing as the instruments themselves. He identified blood cells, both in his own blood and a frog's blood. He noticed that each cell had a dark red spot inside. Later scientists would identify the dot as the center, or nucleus, of the cell.

Leeuwenhoek also looked at some rainwater with his microscope and found animals swimming inside it. These would later be called microorganisms, life that could only be seen with a microscope. He found that the microorganisms were not only in rainwater, however.

Leeuwenhoek scraped a little white matter from his front teeth. When he viewed it with his microscope, he could hardly believe what he saw. There were many tiny animals, similar to those he had seen in rainwater. He estimated that he had more animals living in his mouth than there were people in the Netherlands.

Honor and Disbelief

Friends urged Leeuwenhoek to write to the Royal Society. They were certain that the scientists would be interested in what he had been able to accomplish.

Some members of the Royal Society were jealous of Leeuwenhoek's discoveries. After all, he was uneducated and not even a scientist. In fact, he did not even speak Latin, which was the language of science in

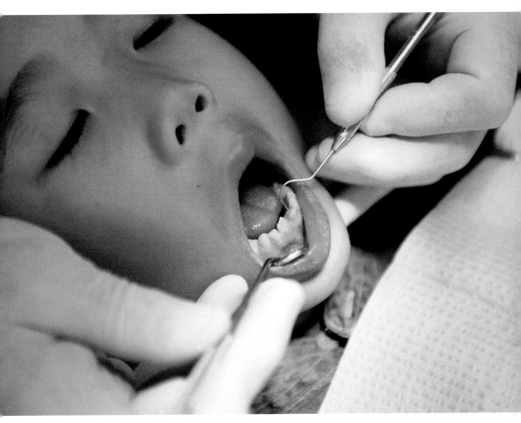

Using his microscope, Leeuwenhoek discovered that plaque scraped from a tooth contains many living organisms.

those days. As a result, some members criticized his work. They accused him of making up a lot of his findings, especially since they could not see the same things with their microscopes.

But most of the members of the Royal Society were highly impressed with Leeuwenhoek's work. The idea that tiny animals were living in rainwater and in one's mouth was something they had never suspected. They urged him to send more of his findings to the society. For fifty years, Leeuwenhoek continued to

The discoveries of Antonie van Leeuwenhoek formed the beginnings of modern medicine.

send drawings and letters about each new thing he found. Many of his discoveries would lay the groundwork for modern medicine. It is no wonder that Leeuwenhoek is still considered the most important microscope user who ever lived.

Building on Leeuwenhoek's Ideas

Over the next hundred years, microscopes continued to improve and so did ways of using them. Scientists built microscopes that could be adjusted and focused to make a sharper picture. They invented razor-sharp tools to cut thin slivers of material to be viewed. Scientists also learned that by adding certain dyes, parts of the **specimen** would be easier to see under the microscope.

During the nineteenth century these microscopes helped scientists find answers to some difficult questions. One of the most important scientists was a French doctor named Louis Pasteur.

In 1864 Pasteur was asked to look into a big problem puzzling French winemakers. For some reason, many of their wines had developed a bitter taste. Pasteur looked at samples of good- and bad-tasting wine under his microscope. The bitter-tasting wine had many microorganisms in it, but only a few were in the good-tasting wine. Pasteur told the winemakers that microorganisms, which he called germs, were making the wine taste bitter.

A Step Further

Pasteur's discovery of what germs could do led other scientists to ask new questions. If tiny germs could damage wine, could they cause illness in animals, too? Various scientists explored the question in different ways.

One scientist, Robert Koch, was curious about **anthrax**, a disease that killed many sheep and cattle. It seemed to spread quickly through herds, and no one knew how to stop it. Looking under his microscope at the blood of a sheep that had died of

Magnified anthrax bacteria. Robert Koch was the first to study anthrax found in sheep's blood.

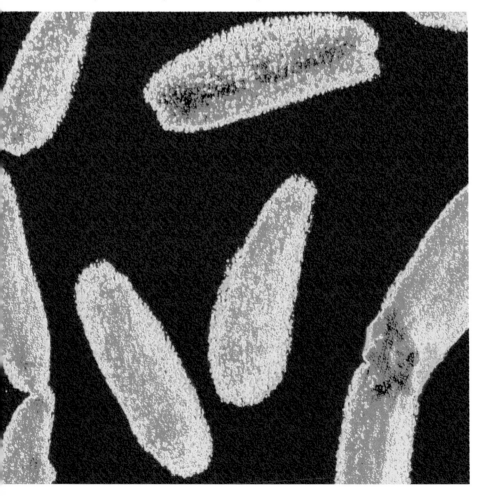

Microscopes

anthrax, he saw long rod-shaped germs. Those germs were not present in the blood of healthy sheep. Koch found the same rod-shaped germs in the soil where sheep infected with anthrax had been buried.

His research showed that the germs continued to live even after the sheep had died. This meant that healthy animals could be infected just by walking on the soil or eating grass in the area of the buried sheep. Koch's work helped farmers. From then on, they knew they should burn the bodies of sheep that had died. That would kill the germs and keep the other sheep healthy.

Germs in the Hospital

Another scientist who was interested in Pasteur's work was a Scottish surgeon named Joseph Lister. His hospital, like others of the nineteenth century, had a very high death rate. About 50 percent of the people who entered the hospital as patients died. Even people with broken bones often became sick and died in the hospital.

Lister wondered if germs were the cause. In those days, doctors rarely washed their hands between patients. Doctors' gowns were often covered with blood and stains. Perhaps, he thought, germs were being spread by the doctors, too.

Lister tried an experiment. He ordered all doctors at the hospital to wash their hands after caring for a patient. They needed to change soiled gowns and

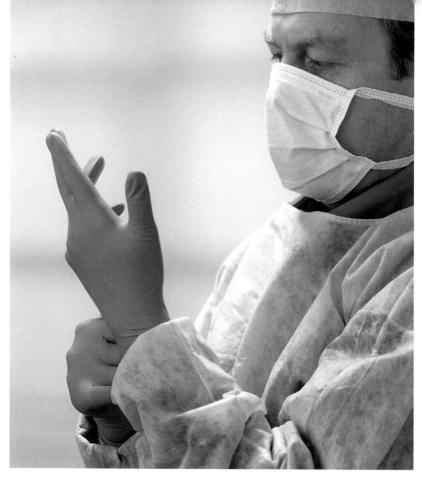

After scrubbing his hands, a surgeon suits up in sterile clothing to prevent the spread of germs.

wash the surgical instruments between patients, too. The results were amazing. The death rate dropped dramatically, from 50 percent to 15 percent. It seemed the germs Pasteur had seen under his microscope were responsible for human illness, too.

As more scientists with microscopes studied diseases, they paved the way for others to find cures or medicines that could control germs. There seemed to be no limits to what microscopes could do in the hands of talented scientists.

Chapter 3

New Kinds of Microscopes

Pasteur, Koch, Lister, and other scientists proved the importance of the microscope. Using the best microscopes of the time, they saw the tiny germs that caused many diseases. There were still some things that they could not see, however.

Smaller than Germs?

Many diseases were caused by **microorganisms**, or germs. But some diseases puzzled scientists. Rabies, a deadly disease passed through the bite of an animal, was one of these puzzles. No microorganisms seemed to cause the disease.

Pasteur himself studied it during the late nineteenth century. He looked at the blood of a dog that had died of rabies. He looked at the saliva, too. But he did not find any germs that caused rabies. Pasteur thought that perhaps there were other things that caused disease. They were similar to germs, he thought, but were far too small to be seen with the microscope.

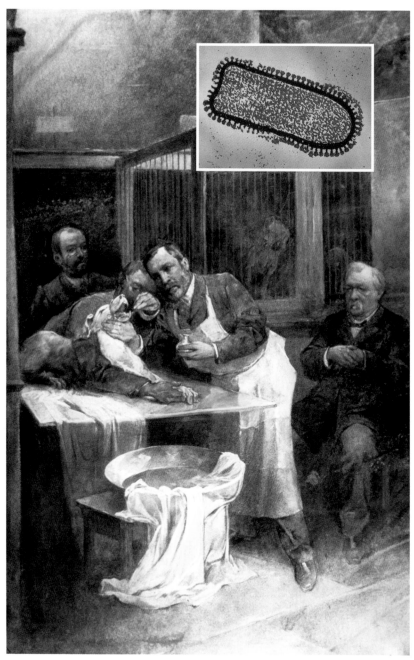

A drawing depicts Louis Pasteur conducting an experiment on a rabid dog. His microscopes were not strong enough to magnify the rabies virus (inset).

Other scientists agreed with Pasteur. Several diseases affecting both plants and animals seemed to be caused by these invisible germs. One doctor termed them **viruses**, which means "poisons." But knowing that diseases such as rabies were caused by viruses was not enough. How could scientists work toward killing viruses unless they could see them?

The best microscopes of Pasteur's day could magnify objects almost two thousand times. But the microscope seemed to have reached its limit. The problem was that microscopes used light waves to study objects. But light waves were not powerful enough to make tinier things, such as viruses, visible.

Better than Light

The answer to this problem did not come from doctors or makers of microscopes. Instead, it came from people who were studying physics, the science of matter and energy. Physicists had discovered that tiny particles called electrons moved in waves. Electron waves are more powerful than light waves. That raised a question with the scientists: Could electron waves be used in a microscope instead of light?

In 1931 scientists in Germany built the first **electron microscope**. They called it a supermicroscope because it was almost eight feet high. It worked by shooting a beam of electrons at the object. The scientists focused the beam by using magnets. The first images were somewhat blurry, but over time the electron microscope would be improved.

Parts of a Microscope

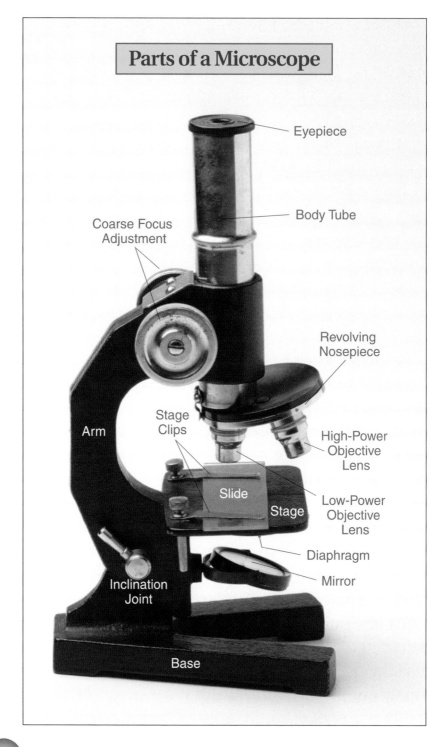

Eyepiece

Body Tube

Coarse Focus Adjustment

Revolving Nosepiece

Arm

Stage Clips

High-Power Objective Lens

Slide

Low-Power Objective Lens

Stage

Diaphragm

Inclination Joint

Mirror

Base

The news of the electron microscope was exciting. Soon scientists all over the world were trying to build their own electron microscopes. They found ways to make the microscope less bulky. They also became more skilled at focusing the beam of electrons. By the mid-1930s many electron microscopes were used in laboratories around the world. Scientists called this improved microscope the transmission electron microscope (TEM). As its name suggests, electron beams pass, or are transmitted, through the object being viewed.

What the TEM Showed

The images seen with the TEM were breathtaking. Some of the best TEMs could magnify an image five hundred thousand times. Scientists could see the details within plant and animal cells. They could even see some molecules.

Medical researchers instantly saw the benefits of using the TEM, too. They could finally see viruses, which they learned were so small that it would take a billion of them to fill a ping pong ball. It is no wonder that they could not be seen with a light microscope. With the power of the TEM, scientists also identified DNA, the substance that contains genetic information that is passed from parent to child at birth.

However, there were drawbacks to the TEM. It could not be used to view live specimens. When the TEM was turned on, all air was pumped out of the microscope to keep the picture sharp. Without air, the cells or other live specimens quickly died. Another drawback was that any specimen must be extremely thin. Getting such thin slices of a specimen was difficult, and the image in the TEM was rather flat.

The transmission electron microscope (TEM) allows scientists to magnify objects five hundred thousand times their normal size.

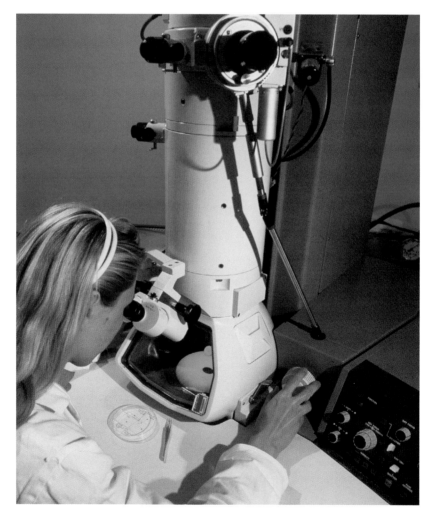

A magnified view of a spider's fangs. The scanning electron microscope allows researchers to view objects three-dimensionally.

The Scanning Electron Microscope

Scientists worked hard to improve the TEM. In 1960 they built what they called the scanning electron microscope (SEM). It works in a different way than the TEM. Instead of shooting beams of electrons at a specimen, the SEM's electrons scan only the outside of an object. Once they hit, the electrons bounce off. A computer in the SEM reads the patterns of the scattering electrons. Then it displays the shape of the object on a viewing screen.

The SEM does not magnify objects as much as the TEM. But its image is three-dimensional instead of flat. The SEM does not require specimens to be ultra-thin, either. That is because the microscope scans the entire object rather than just a slice of it.

There are advantages to seeing an entire specimen. Medical doctors can view a blood cell, for example, and study it from any angle. Researchers have used the SEM to get three-dimensional views of brain cells. This has helped them understand more about Alzheimer's disease and other causes of memory loss. They have looked at images of heart cells, too. Doctors want to learn more about what happens to cell walls after a person has a stroke or a heart attack.

But medical scientists are not the only ones who are learning things from the SEM. Textile makers can look at the threads of fabrics with the SEM. That can help them understand why certain dyes work with

Every detail of a wasp's head can be seen through today's advanced microscopes.

some materials and not others. Builders also can examine metal and cement with the SEM. Looking at molecules of those materials, they can see what causes them to crumble or crack.

Although the SEM has been an exciting tool for scientists, it is not the most modern microscope. Since its invention in 1960, scientists have continued their search for ways to see into the world of the ultrasmall.

Chapter 4

A Microscopic Future

Electron microscopes could see amazing details. But scientists found that electron waves damaged or killed living specimens, such as cells. This was a problem for doctors. They wanted to learn about how certain **bacteria** behaved. But how could they observe this behavior if the specimens were no longer alive?

Seeing with Sound

One solution was the **acoustic microscope**. It uses sound waves instead of electron or light waves. The sound waves are very powerful, vibrating at 1 billion cycles per second. They bounce off the specimen and create echoes. A sensitive computer then creates a picture based on the pattern of echoes.

The acoustic microscope has many advantages. One important advantage is that sound waves can "see" through solid material. A researcher who wants to view a tiny microchip working inside a computer can use an acoustic microscope to do that. It is not necessary to take the microchip out or to cut a thin slice of it.

Doctors who treat people with cancer also like this new microscope. They can study the effects of cancer on their patients' blood cells and bones. This may tell doctors if a certain treatment is working. They can also use the microscope to do a biopsy, which closely looks at tissue to see if a person has cancer. In the

An acoustic microscope provides magnification through sound waves.

past, a doctor had to remove tissue and study it. But with the acoustic microscope, the doctor does not need to do any cutting. The microscope can see if there is cancer in the tissue.

Seeing Atoms

Another improvement in microscopes has made them more powerful. Scientists were amazed when they first could see molecules with the TEM. But a new type of electron microscope has allowed scientists to see far smaller particles than molecules. They can see individual atoms, which are particles so small that 16 million of them could fit on the head of a pin.

This new instrument is called the scanning tunneling microscope (STM). Like the SEM, it shows the surface of an object rather than the inside. It uses a very sensitive needle that is controlled by a computer. The computer notices the tiny changes in the electron waves between the needle tip and the object. The computer uses this information to create the image on a screen.

The STM can magnify the object 500 million times, which is enough magnification to see individual atoms. It also can show the best-ever image of viruses and DNA strands.

Helping Babies Breathe

One group of doctors is using the STM to learn more about the lungs. They know that healthy lungs move

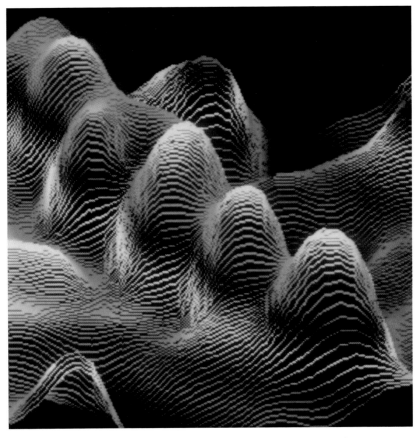

A strand of DNA is magnified two and a half million times (pictured). The scanning tunneling microscope is capable of magnifying objects five hundred million times.

in and out easily. Every time a person takes a breath, the lungs expand. But the lungs of many premature babies do not expand as they should. Often, these babies have trouble breathing and die.

With the STM, doctors have seen that there is a chemical substance in lung tissue. They know that this substance is not present in many premature babies. Doctors hope that by studying the molecules

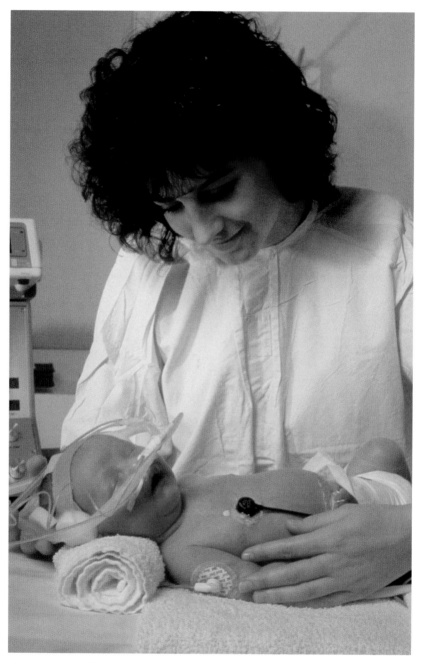

A nurse tends to a premature baby. Research with the STM may give doctors new tools for treating problems connected with early birth.

of this mysterious chemical, they can learn to make it themselves. Perhaps in the future, scientists can make a drug that can give these babies the chemical they need to breathe.

Micromachines

The STM has also helped scientists create tiny new machines, called micromachines. The most common micromachine is a **microchip**, which can be found in every computer. Microchips store information. They also control the way a computer works.

Looking at an enlarged view of a microchip is like seeing a very complicated maze. Most microchips are less than one-quarter of an inch square. On each chip there may be as many as 3 million components, or parts. It is hard to imagine how anyone could create such a complex system of electrical pathways.

Some complicated machines can be even smaller than a microchip. In fact, scientists have already built tiny motors and other machines that are thinner than a human hair. They hope that such machines can be useful in the future, especially in medicine. One might be a hearing aid so small that it would be almost invisible. Another might be programmed to destroy cancer cells before they can do any harm.

Some machines would be important for the environment, too. Perhaps some machines could be used to eat garbage from landfills. Others could be released after a chemical spill. The machines could remove harmful substances so that they do not poison the water, air, or soil.

The Tiniest Microscope

Although these machines are just in the experimental stage, scientists think they offer great possibilities

A tiny camera, seen in inset in the throat, allows a doctor to see inside a patient's body. A microscope might someday do the same.

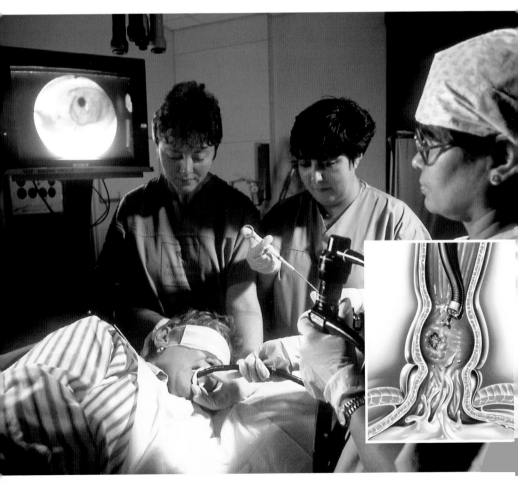

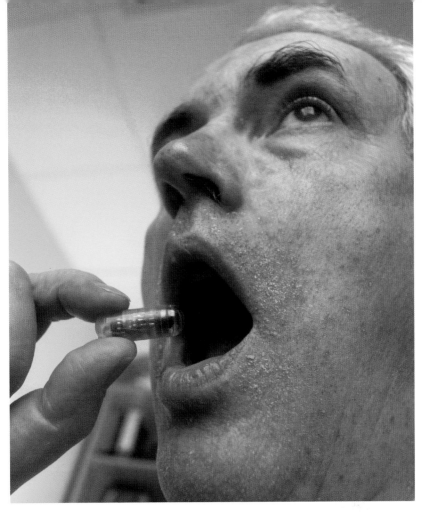

A microscope inside a pill could provide vivid images of a patient's stomach just as this microcamera in a pill does now.

for the future. But there is a tiny machine that scientists are working on today. Not only was it built by using powerful microscopes, but it is itself a microscope. Scientists at the University of California at Berkeley are developing the first micromicroscope. It is smaller than the head of a pin.

The little instrument will be as powerful as an electron microscope. But it will be as harmless to living specimens as an acoustic microscope. The

A micromachine (left) is tinier than a coin (right). Developers are working to create a microscope that will be even smaller than this micromachine.

new microscope will be very helpful to doctors who treat people with cancer. By guiding the microscope inside the patient, doctors will be able to see exactly where the cancer cells are spreading. They also will be able to use the microscope to observe the effects of certain drugs on cancer cells. By seeing the changes inside the cell, doctors will know right away if a drug is working.

Developers think that their micromicroscope can help in the war on terrorism, too. It will be able to see molecules of smallpox, anthrax, and other dangerous substances, which will help investigators identify terrorist targets. These substances can then be destroyed before they can make people sick.

Looking Ahead

Microscopes have come a long way. The early magnifiers allowed people to see details on an insect's wing. Today's microscopes can show far more. Some can show the cells in the wing; others can observe strands of DNA in those same cells.

No one is sure how much more powerful tomorrow's microscopes can be. But one thing is certain: There will always be a scientist somewhere trying to make a microscope that is smaller, or more powerful, or easier to use. Scientists have always had a desire to explore the world and learn why things are the way they are. Microscopes are the most important tool for answering those questions.

acoustic microscope: A microscope that uses sound waves to make a magnified image of an object.

anthrax: A deadly disease that can infect both animals and humans.

bacteria: Tiny living things that can only be seen with a microscope. Some bacteria cause disease.

cell: The small units from which all living things are made. Cells were first noticed under a microscope by Robert Hooke.

compound microscope: A microscope that uses light waves and two or more lenses to make a magnified image of an object.

concave lens: A piece of curved glass that is thinner in the middle and thicker at the edges.

convex lens: A piece of curved glass that is thicker in the middle and thinner at the edges.

electron microscope: A microscope that uses beams of charged particles (electrons) instead of light waves to make a magnified image of an object.

microorganism: A tiny living thing that can only be seen through a microscope.

microchip: A tiny machine containing thousands of electronic pathways. Microchips are used to help run computers and other electronic equipment.

simple microscope: A microscope that can magnify an object using only one lens.

specimen: A sample viewed under a microscope.

virus: A tiny microorganism that is smaller than bacteria and can cause disease.

For Further Exploration

Beverly Birch, *Pasteur's Fight Against Microbes.* Hauppauge, NY: Barron's Educational Series, 1996. This book provides excellent details of Pasteur's use of a microscope to form new ideas about disease.

David Darling, *Micromachines and Nanotechnology: The Amazing New World of the Ultrasmall.* Parsippany, NJ: Dillon, 1995. Although challenging for some readers, this book offers good detail on the way the STM has helped scientists develop smaller machines.

Kenneth Raines, *Guide to Microlife.* New York: Franklin Watts, 1996. The author uses good photographs and helpful explanations of how microorganisms interact with other forms of life.

Ranger Rick, "Here's How an Electron Microscope Works," November 1997. A simple explanation of a complicated tool.

Howard Tomb and Dennis Kunkel, *Microaliens: Dazzling Journeys with an Electron Microscope.* New York: Farrar, Straus, and Giroux, 1993. This book presents amazing photographs of images through the most powerful of today's microscopes.

Lisa Yount, *Antonie van Leeuwenhoek: First to See Microscopic Life.* Springfield, NJ: Enslow, 1996. This text includes helpful bibliographical notes.

Index